Disappearing Dinosaurs

Contents   **Page**

written by Pam Holden

Why did the dinosaurs disappear from Earth? Lots of different ideas have been given, but nobody knows for sure. These amazing creatures disappeared long before people began to live on Earth. They have been gone for millions of years!

We are now beginning to learn some things about their life here. This is because the bones of dinosaurs have been found in many countries in the past 350 years. Skeletons have been found preserved as fossils in rocks and swamps.

The bones and body parts are studied by scientists called paleontologists, who learn new facts about dinosaurs. They rebuild the old skeletons to show what the many different kinds looked like.

We now know more about their size and shape, what they ate, and how they moved. Many facts are known, but still nobody can be sure how or why they disappeared.

Did the dinosaurs all disappear because of a sudden change in the world's climate? Was the world suddenly too cold or too hot for them to survive? One idea is that huge glaciers spread out and covered Earth's surface, making it too cold for anything to grow.

If plants could no longer grow, then all the plant-eaters would have starved and died out. There would have been nothing left for the meat-eaters to hunt for food.

Some scientists think that giant volcanoes may have made the Earth too cool. Gas from volcanic eruptions, as well as dust in the air and the oceans, would have blocked the sunlight.

Enormous fires and storms would have made Earth an impossible place for the dinosaurs to survive. Scientists can research this idea by studying deep craters left in Earth's surface by eruptions.

Did the mighty dinosaurs become extinct because burning comets or meteors crashed to Earth and destroyed their habitat?

If all plant life was burnt away by chunks of red-hot rock, the dinosaurs' food chain would have quickly broken down, leaving them to starve to death.

Some paleontologists think that the answer might be in the stars. An exploding star, called a supernova, may have made an enormous cloud of fall-out that was deadly for all life on Earth.

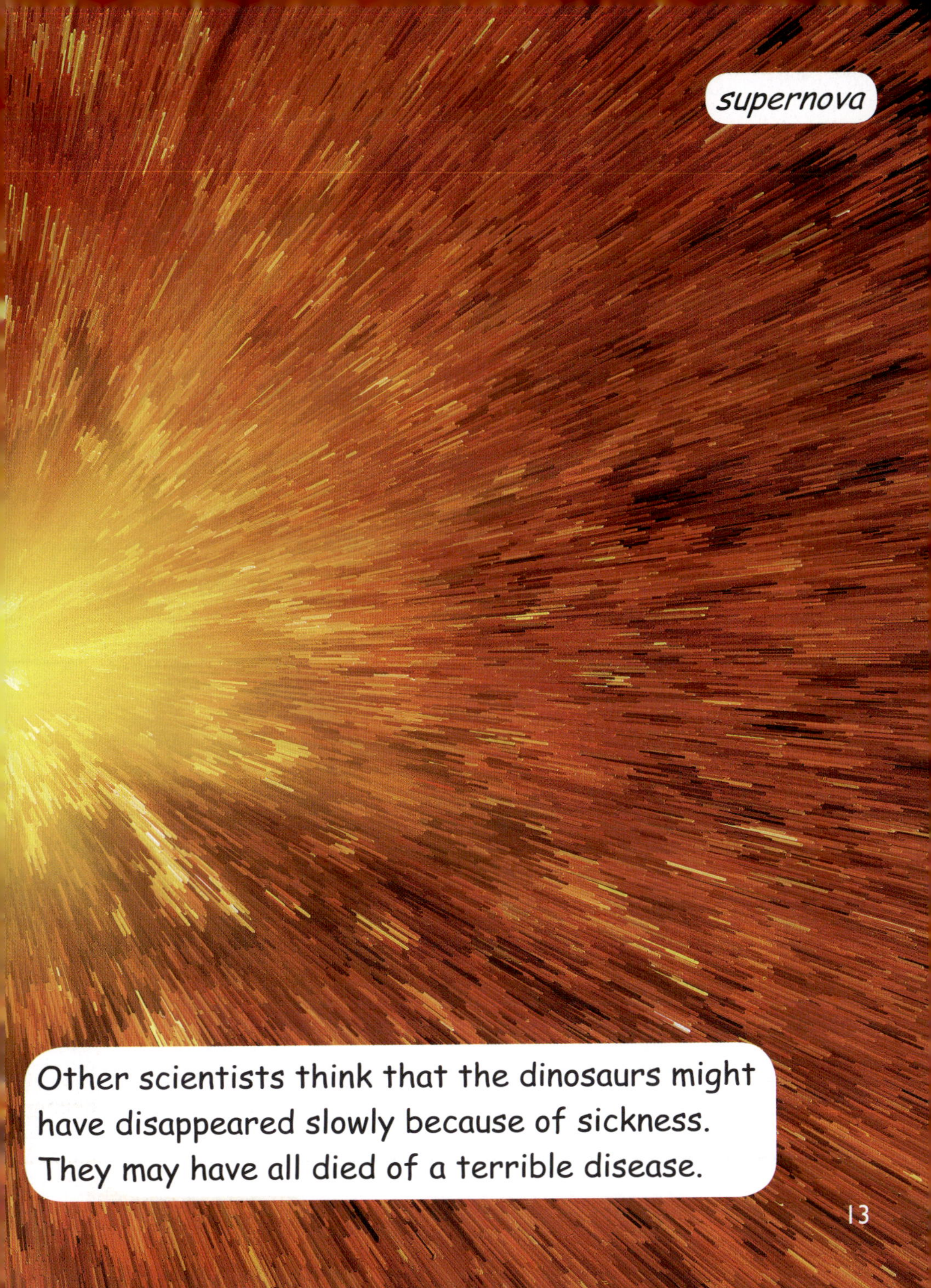

Other scientists think that the dinosaurs might have disappeared slowly because of sickness. They may have all died of a terrible disease.

Another idea is that the fierce, greedy meat-eaters ate so many plant-eaters that they didn't have enough food left to survive. Scientists are still not sure whether the dinosaurs died out suddenly or slowly. Did they become extinct because of cold, hunger, heat, or illness?

meat-eaters

As new discoveries are made, more research will be done. One day we might know answers to the mystery. Which idea do you think is most likely to answer our questions? Do you wish that dinosaurs were still living right here on Earth? Why, or why not?